This book belo

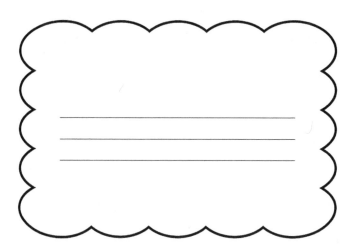

5 tips for secure passwords

- Never use the username, your real name, date of birth or any other personal information as a password.
- Use at least four types of spelling, including upper/lower case, letters, numbers, and special characters such as !@#%$*~;.
- Give the password a length of at least twelve characters.
- Never use the same password for all accounts.
- Change your passwords regularly.

Please don't leave this password book out in the open. Keep it properly stored and tucked away in a safe or vault.

A

VENDOR/WEBSITE	
USER NAME	
PASSWORD/PIN	DATE CHANGED
PASSWORD/PIN	DATE CHANGED
PASSWORD/PIN	DATE CHANGED
📞	
NOTES	

VENDOR/WEBSITE	
USER NAME	
PASSWORD/PIN	DATE CHANGED
PASSWORD/PIN	DATE CHANGED
PASSWORD/PIN	DATE CHANGED
📞	
NOTES	

VENDOR/WEBSITE	
USER NAME	
PASSWORD/PIN	DATE CHANGED
PASSWORD/PIN	DATE CHANGED
PASSWORD/PIN	DATE CHANGED
📞	
NOTES	

VENDOR/WEBSITE	
USER NAME	
PASSWORD/PIN	DATE CHANGED
PASSWORD/PIN	DATE CHANGED
PASSWORD/PIN	DATE CHANGED
📞	
NOTES	

VENDOR/WEBSITE	
USER NAME	
PASSWORD/PIN	DATE CHANGED
PASSWORD/PIN	DATE CHANGED
PASSWORD/PIN	DATE CHANGED
📞	
NOTES	

VENDOR/WEBSITE	
USER NAME	
PASSWORD/PIN	DATE CHANGED
PASSWORD/PIN	DATE CHANGED
PASSWORD/PIN	DATE CHANGED
📞	
NOTES	

VENDOR/WEBSITE	
USER NAME	
PASSWORD/PIN	DATE CHANGED
PASSWORD/PIN	DATE CHANGED
PASSWORD/PIN	DATE CHANGED
📞	
NOTES	

VENDOR/WEBSITE	
USER NAME	
PASSWORD/PIN	DATE CHANGED
PASSWORD/PIN	DATE CHANGED
PASSWORD/PIN	DATE CHANGED
📞	
NOTES	

A

VENDOR/WEBSITE	
USER NAME	
PASSWORD/PIN	DATE CHANGED
PASSWORD/PIN	DATE CHANGED
PASSWORD/PIN	DATE CHANGED
☎	
NOTES	

VENDOR/WEBSITE	
USER NAME	
PASSWORD/PIN	DATE CHANGED
PASSWORD/PIN	DATE CHANGED
PASSWORD/PIN	DATE CHANGED
☎	
NOTES	

VENDOR/WEBSITE	
USER NAME	
PASSWORD/PIN	DATE CHANGED
PASSWORD/PIN	DATE CHANGED
PASSWORD/PIN	DATE CHANGED
☎	
NOTES	

VENDOR/WEBSITE	
USER NAME	
PASSWORD/PIN	DATE CHANGED
PASSWORD/PIN	DATE CHANGED
PASSWORD/PIN	DATE CHANGED
☎	
NOTES	

	A
VENDOR/WEBSITE	
USER NAME	
PASSWORD/PIN	DATE CHANGED
PASSWORD/PIN	DATE CHANGED
PASSWORD/PIN	DATE CHANGED
📞	
NOTES	
VENDOR/WEBSITE	
USER NAME	
PASSWORD/PIN	DATE CHANGED
PASSWORD/PIN	DATE CHANGED
PASSWORD/PIN	DATE CHANGED
📞	
NOTES	
VENDOR/WEBSITE	
USER NAME	
PASSWORD/PIN	DATE CHANGED
PASSWORD/PIN	DATE CHANGED
PASSWORD/PIN	DATE CHANGED
📞	
NOTES	
VENDOR/WEBSITE	
USER NAME	
PASSWORD/PIN	DATE CHANGED
PASSWORD/PIN	DATE CHANGED
PASSWORD/PIN	DATE CHANGED
📞	
NOTES	

B

VENDOR/WEBSITE	
USER NAME	
PASSWORD/PIN	DATE CHANGED
PASSWORD/PIN	DATE CHANGED
PASSWORD/PIN	DATE CHANGED
📞	
NOTES	

VENDOR/WEBSITE	
USER NAME	
PASSWORD/PIN	DATE CHANGED
PASSWORD/PIN	DATE CHANGED
PASSWORD/PIN	DATE CHANGED
📞	
NOTES	

VENDOR/WEBSITE	
USER NAME	
PASSWORD/PIN	DATE CHANGED
PASSWORD/PIN	DATE CHANGED
PASSWORD/PIN	DATE CHANGED
📞	
NOTES	

VENDOR/WEBSITE	
USER NAME	
PASSWORD/PIN	DATE CHANGED
PASSWORD/PIN	DATE CHANGED
PASSWORD/PIN	DATE CHANGED
📞	
NOTES	

	B
VENDOR/WEBSITE	
USER NAME	
PASSWORD/PIN	DATE CHANGED
PASSWORD/PIN	DATE CHANGED
PASSWORD/PIN	DATE CHANGED
☏	
NOTES	
VENDOR/WEBSITE	
USER NAME	
PASSWORD/PIN	DATE CHANGED
PASSWORD/PIN	DATE CHANGED
PASSWORD/PIN	DATE CHANGED
☏	
NOTES	
VENDOR/WEBSITE	
USER NAME	
PASSWORD/PIN	DATE CHANGED
PASSWORD/PIN	DATE CHANGED
PASSWORD/PIN	DATE CHANGED
☏	
NOTES	
VENDOR/WEBSITE	
USER NAME	
PASSWORD/PIN	DATE CHANGED
PASSWORD/PIN	DATE CHANGED
PASSWORD/PIN	DATE CHANGED
☏	
NOTES	

B

VENDOR/WEBSITE	
USER NAME	
PASSWORD/PIN	DATE CHANGED
PASSWORD/PIN	DATE CHANGED
PASSWORD/PIN	DATE CHANGED
NOTES	

VENDOR/WEBSITE	
USER NAME	
PASSWORD/PIN	DATE CHANGED
PASSWORD/PIN	DATE CHANGED
PASSWORD/PIN	DATE CHANGED
NOTES	

VENDOR/WEBSITE	
USER NAME	
PASSWORD/PIN	DATE CHANGED
PASSWORD/PIN	DATE CHANGED
PASSWORD/PIN	DATE CHANGED
NOTES	

VENDOR/WEBSITE	
USER NAME	
PASSWORD/PIN	DATE CHANGED
PASSWORD/PIN	DATE CHANGED
PASSWORD/PIN	DATE CHANGED
NOTES	

	B
VENDOR/WEBSITE	
USER NAME	
PASSWORD/PIN	DATE CHANGED
PASSWORD/PIN	DATE CHANGED
PASSWORD/PIN	DATE CHANGED
📞	
NOTES	
VENDOR/WEBSITE	
USER NAME	
PASSWORD/PIN	DATE CHANGED
PASSWORD/PIN	DATE CHANGED
PASSWORD/PIN	DATE CHANGED
📞	
NOTES	
VENDOR/WEBSITE	
USER NAME	
PASSWORD/PIN	DATE CHANGED
PASSWORD/PIN	DATE CHANGED
PASSWORD/PIN	DATE CHANGED
📞	
NOTES	
VENDOR/WEBSITE	
USER NAME	
PASSWORD/PIN	DATE CHANGED
PASSWORD/PIN	DATE CHANGED
PASSWORD/PIN	DATE CHANGED
📞	
NOTES	

C

VENDOR/WEBSITE	
USER NAME	
PASSWORD/PIN	DATE CHANGED
PASSWORD/PIN	DATE CHANGED
PASSWORD/PIN	DATE CHANGED
📞	
NOTES	

VENDOR/WEBSITE	
USER NAME	
PASSWORD/PIN	DATE CHANGED
PASSWORD/PIN	DATE CHANGED
PASSWORD/PIN	DATE CHANGED
📞	
NOTES	

VENDOR/WEBSITE	
USER NAME	
PASSWORD/PIN	DATE CHANGED
PASSWORD/PIN	DATE CHANGED
PASSWORD/PIN	DATE CHANGED
📞	
NOTES	

VENDOR/WEBSITE	
USER NAME	
PASSWORD/PIN	DATE CHANGED
PASSWORD/PIN	DATE CHANGED
PASSWORD/PIN	DATE CHANGED
📞	
NOTES	

VENDOR/WEBSITE	
USER NAME	
PASSWORD/PIN	DATE CHANGED
PASSWORD/PIN	DATE CHANGED
PASSWORD/PIN	DATE CHANGED
NOTES	
VENDOR/WEBSITE	
USER NAME	
PASSWORD/PIN	DATE CHANGED
PASSWORD/PIN	DATE CHANGED
PASSWORD/PIN	DATE CHANGED
NOTES	
VENDOR/WEBSITE	
USER NAME	
PASSWORD/PIN	DATE CHANGED
PASSWORD/PIN	DATE CHANGED
PASSWORD/PIN	DATE CHANGED
NOTES	
VENDOR/WEBSITE	
USER NAME	
PASSWORD/PIN	DATE CHANGED
PASSWORD/PIN	DATE CHANGED
PASSWORD/PIN	DATE CHANGED
NOTES	

C

VENDOR/WEBSITE	
USER NAME	
PASSWORD/PIN	DATE CHANGED
PASSWORD/PIN	DATE CHANGED
PASSWORD/PIN	DATE CHANGED
☎	
NOTES	

VENDOR/WEBSITE	
USER NAME	
PASSWORD/PIN	DATE CHANGED
PASSWORD/PIN	DATE CHANGED
PASSWORD/PIN	DATE CHANGED
☎	
NOTES	

VENDOR/WEBSITE	
USER NAME	
PASSWORD/PIN	DATE CHANGED
PASSWORD/PIN	DATE CHANGED
PASSWORD/PIN	DATE CHANGED
☎	
NOTES	

VENDOR/WEBSITE	
USER NAME	
PASSWORD/PIN	DATE CHANGED
PASSWORD/PIN	DATE CHANGED
PASSWORD/PIN	DATE CHANGED
☎	
NOTES	

	C
VENDOR/WEBSITE	
USER NAME	
PASSWORD/PIN	DATE CHANGED
PASSWORD/PIN	DATE CHANGED
PASSWORD/PIN	DATE CHANGED
📞	
NOTES	
VENDOR/WEBSITE	
USER NAME	
PASSWORD/PIN	DATE CHANGED
PASSWORD/PIN	DATE CHANGED
PASSWORD/PIN	DATE CHANGED
📞	
NOTES	
VENDOR/WEBSITE	
USER NAME	
PASSWORD/PIN	DATE CHANGED
PASSWORD/PIN	DATE CHANGED
PASSWORD/PIN	DATE CHANGED
📞	
NOTES	
VENDOR/WEBSITE	
USER NAME	
PASSWORD/PIN	DATE CHANGED
PASSWORD/PIN	DATE CHANGED
PASSWORD/PIN	DATE CHANGED
📞	
NOTES	

D

VENDOR/WEBSITE	
USER NAME	
PASSWORD/PIN	DATE CHANGED
PASSWORD/PIN	DATE CHANGED
PASSWORD/PIN	DATE CHANGED
📞	
NOTES	

VENDOR/WEBSITE	
USER NAME	
PASSWORD/PIN	DATE CHANGED
PASSWORD/PIN	DATE CHANGED
PASSWORD/PIN	DATE CHANGED
📞	
NOTES	

VENDOR/WEBSITE	
USER NAME	
PASSWORD/PIN	DATE CHANGED
PASSWORD/PIN	DATE CHANGED
PASSWORD/PIN	DATE CHANGED
📞	
NOTES	

VENDOR/WEBSITE	
USER NAME	
PASSWORD/PIN	DATE CHANGED
PASSWORD/PIN	DATE CHANGED
PASSWORD/PIN	DATE CHANGED
📞	
NOTES	

	D
VENDOR/WEBSITE	
USER NAME	
PASSWORD/PIN	DATE CHANGED
PASSWORD/PIN	DATE CHANGED
PASSWORD/PIN	DATE CHANGED
NOTES	
VENDOR/WEBSITE	
USER NAME	
PASSWORD/PIN	DATE CHANGED
PASSWORD/PIN	DATE CHANGED
PASSWORD/PIN	DATE CHANGED
NOTES	
VENDOR/WEBSITE	
USER NAME	
PASSWORD/PIN	DATE CHANGED
PASSWORD/PIN	DATE CHANGED
PASSWORD/PIN	DATE CHANGED
NOTES	
VENDOR/WEBSITE	
USER NAME	
PASSWORD/PIN	DATE CHANGED
PASSWORD/PIN	DATE CHANGED
PASSWORD/PIN	DATE CHANGED
NOTES	

D

VENDOR/WEBSITE	
USER NAME	
PASSWORD/PIN	DATE CHANGED
PASSWORD/PIN	DATE CHANGED
PASSWORD/PIN	DATE CHANGED
☎	
NOTES	

VENDOR/WEBSITE	
USER NAME	
PASSWORD/PIN	DATE CHANGED
PASSWORD/PIN	DATE CHANGED
PASSWORD/PIN	DATE CHANGED
☎	
NOTES	

VENDOR/WEBSITE	
USER NAME	
PASSWORD/PIN	DATE CHANGED
PASSWORD/PIN	DATE CHANGED
PASSWORD/PIN	DATE CHANGED
☎	
NOTES	

VENDOR/WEBSITE	
USER NAME	
PASSWORD/PIN	DATE CHANGED
PASSWORD/PIN	DATE CHANGED
PASSWORD/PIN	DATE CHANGED
☎	
NOTES	

	D
VENDOR/WEBSITE	
USER NAME	
PASSWORD/PIN	DATE CHANGED
PASSWORD/PIN	DATE CHANGED
PASSWORD/PIN	DATE CHANGED
📞	
NOTES	
VENDOR/WEBSITE	
USER NAME	
PASSWORD/PIN	DATE CHANGED
PASSWORD/PIN	DATE CHANGED
PASSWORD/PIN	DATE CHANGED
📞	
NOTES	
VENDOR/WEBSITE	
USER NAME	
PASSWORD/PIN	DATE CHANGED
PASSWORD/PIN	DATE CHANGED
PASSWORD/PIN	DATE CHANGED
📞	
NOTES	
VENDOR/WEBSITE	
USER NAME	
PASSWORD/PIN	DATE CHANGED
PASSWORD/PIN	DATE CHANGED
PASSWORD/PIN	DATE CHANGED
📞	
NOTES	

E

VENDOR/WEBSITE	
USER NAME	
PASSWORD/PIN	DATE CHANGED
PASSWORD/PIN	DATE CHANGED
PASSWORD/PIN	DATE CHANGED
📞	
NOTES	

VENDOR/WEBSITE	
USER NAME	
PASSWORD/PIN	DATE CHANGED
PASSWORD/PIN	DATE CHANGED
PASSWORD/PIN	DATE CHANGED
📞	
NOTES	

VENDOR/WEBSITE	
USER NAME	
PASSWORD/PIN	DATE CHANGED
PASSWORD/PIN	DATE CHANGED
PASSWORD/PIN	DATE CHANGED
📞	
NOTES	

VENDOR/WEBSITE	
USER NAME	
PASSWORD/PIN	DATE CHANGED
PASSWORD/PIN	DATE CHANGED
PASSWORD/PIN	DATE CHANGED
📞	
NOTES	

	E
VENDOR/WEBSITE	
USER NAME	
PASSWORD/PIN	DATE CHANGED
PASSWORD/PIN	DATE CHANGED
PASSWORD/PIN	DATE CHANGED
NOTES	

VENDOR/WEBSITE	
USER NAME	
PASSWORD/PIN	DATE CHANGED
PASSWORD/PIN	DATE CHANGED
PASSWORD/PIN	DATE CHANGED
NOTES	

VENDOR/WEBSITE	
USER NAME	
PASSWORD/PIN	DATE CHANGED
PASSWORD/PIN	DATE CHANGED
PASSWORD/PIN	DATE CHANGED
NOTES	

VENDOR/WEBSITE	
USER NAME	
PASSWORD/PIN	DATE CHANGED
PASSWORD/PIN	DATE CHANGED
PASSWORD/PIN	DATE CHANGED
NOTES	

E

VENDOR/WEBSITE	
USER NAME	
PASSWORD/PIN	DATE CHANGED
PASSWORD/PIN	DATE CHANGED
PASSWORD/PIN	DATE CHANGED
📞	
NOTES	

VENDOR/WEBSITE	
USER NAME	
PASSWORD/PIN	DATE CHANGED
PASSWORD/PIN	DATE CHANGED
PASSWORD/PIN	DATE CHANGED
📞	
NOTES	

VENDOR/WEBSITE	
USER NAME	
PASSWORD/PIN	DATE CHANGED
PASSWORD/PIN	DATE CHANGED
PASSWORD/PIN	DATE CHANGED
📞	
NOTES	

VENDOR/WEBSITE	
USER NAME	
PASSWORD/PIN	DATE CHANGED
PASSWORD/PIN	DATE CHANGED
PASSWORD/PIN	DATE CHANGED
📞	
NOTES	

VENDOR/WEBSITE	
USER NAME	
PASSWORD/PIN	DATE CHANGED
PASSWORD/PIN	DATE CHANGED
PASSWORD/PIN	DATE CHANGED
☎	
NOTES	

VENDOR/WEBSITE	
USER NAME	
PASSWORD/PIN	DATE CHANGED
PASSWORD/PIN	DATE CHANGED
PASSWORD/PIN	DATE CHANGED
☎	
NOTES	

VENDOR/WEBSITE	
USER NAME	
PASSWORD/PIN	DATE CHANGED
PASSWORD/PIN	DATE CHANGED
PASSWORD/PIN	DATE CHANGED
☎	
NOTES	

VENDOR/WEBSITE	
USER NAME	
PASSWORD/PIN	DATE CHANGED
PASSWORD/PIN	DATE CHANGED
PASSWORD/PIN	DATE CHANGED
☎	
NOTES	

F

VENDOR/WEBSITE	
USER NAME	
PASSWORD/PIN	DATE CHANGED
PASSWORD/PIN	DATE CHANGED
PASSWORD/PIN	DATE CHANGED
☎	
NOTES	

VENDOR/WEBSITE	
USER NAME	
PASSWORD/PIN	DATE CHANGED
PASSWORD/PIN	DATE CHANGED
PASSWORD/PIN	DATE CHANGED
☎	
NOTES	

VENDOR/WEBSITE	
USER NAME	
PASSWORD/PIN	DATE CHANGED
PASSWORD/PIN	DATE CHANGED
PASSWORD/PIN	DATE CHANGED
☎	
NOTES	

VENDOR/WEBSITE	
USER NAME	
PASSWORD/PIN	DATE CHANGED
PASSWORD/PIN	DATE CHANGED
PASSWORD/PIN	DATE CHANGED
☎	
NOTES	

	F
VENDOR/WEBSITE	
USER NAME	
PASSWORD/PIN	DATE CHANGED
PASSWORD/PIN	DATE CHANGED
PASSWORD/PIN	DATE CHANGED
📞	
NOTES	
VENDOR/WEBSITE	
USER NAME	
PASSWORD/PIN	DATE CHANGED
PASSWORD/PIN	DATE CHANGED
PASSWORD/PIN	DATE CHANGED
📞	
NOTES	
VENDOR/WEBSITE	
USER NAME	
PASSWORD/PIN	DATE CHANGED
PASSWORD/PIN	DATE CHANGED
PASSWORD/PIN	DATE CHANGED
📞	
NOTES	
VENDOR/WEBSITE	
USER NAME	
PASSWORD/PIN	DATE CHANGED
PASSWORD/PIN	DATE CHANGED
PASSWORD/PIN	DATE CHANGED
📞	
NOTES	

F

VENDOR/WEBSITE	
USER NAME	
PASSWORD/PIN	DATE CHANGED
PASSWORD/PIN	DATE CHANGED
PASSWORD/PIN	DATE CHANGED
📞	
NOTES	

VENDOR/WEBSITE	
USER NAME	
PASSWORD/PIN	DATE CHANGED
PASSWORD/PIN	DATE CHANGED
PASSWORD/PIN	DATE CHANGED
📞	
NOTES	

VENDOR/WEBSITE	
USER NAME	
PASSWORD/PIN	DATE CHANGED
PASSWORD/PIN	DATE CHANGED
PASSWORD/PIN	DATE CHANGED
📞	
NOTES	

VENDOR/WEBSITE	
USER NAME	
PASSWORD/PIN	DATE CHANGED
PASSWORD/PIN	DATE CHANGED
PASSWORD/PIN	DATE CHANGED
📞	
NOTES	

VENDOR/WEBSITE	
USER NAME	
PASSWORD/PIN	DATE CHANGED
PASSWORD/PIN	DATE CHANGED
PASSWORD/PIN	DATE CHANGED
📞	
NOTES	
VENDOR/WEBSITE	
USER NAME	
PASSWORD/PIN	DATE CHANGED
PASSWORD/PIN	DATE CHANGED
PASSWORD/PIN	DATE CHANGED
📞	
NOTES	
VENDOR/WEBSITE	
USER NAME	
PASSWORD/PIN	DATE CHANGED
PASSWORD/PIN	DATE CHANGED
PASSWORD/PIN	DATE CHANGED
📞	
NOTES	
VENDOR/WEBSITE	
USER NAME	
PASSWORD/PIN	DATE CHANGED
PASSWORD/PIN	DATE CHANGED
PASSWORD/PIN	DATE CHANGED
📞	
NOTES	

G

VENDOR/WEBSITE	
USER NAME	
PASSWORD/PIN	DATE CHANGED
PASSWORD/PIN	DATE CHANGED
PASSWORD/PIN	DATE CHANGED
📞	
NOTES	

VENDOR/WEBSITE	
USER NAME	
PASSWORD/PIN	DATE CHANGED
PASSWORD/PIN	DATE CHANGED
PASSWORD/PIN	DATE CHANGED
📞	
NOTES	

VENDOR/WEBSITE	
USER NAME	
PASSWORD/PIN	DATE CHANGED
PASSWORD/PIN	DATE CHANGED
PASSWORD/PIN	DATE CHANGED
📞	
NOTES	

VENDOR/WEBSITE	
USER NAME	
PASSWORD/PIN	DATE CHANGED
PASSWORD/PIN	DATE CHANGED
PASSWORD/PIN	DATE CHANGED
📞	
NOTES	

VENDOR/WEBSITE	
USER NAME	
PASSWORD/PIN	DATE CHANGED
PASSWORD/PIN	DATE CHANGED
PASSWORD/PIN	DATE CHANGED
📞	
NOTES	

VENDOR/WEBSITE	
USER NAME	
PASSWORD/PIN	DATE CHANGED
PASSWORD/PIN	DATE CHANGED
PASSWORD/PIN	DATE CHANGED
📞	
NOTES	

VENDOR/WEBSITE	
USER NAME	
PASSWORD/PIN	DATE CHANGED
PASSWORD/PIN	DATE CHANGED
PASSWORD/PIN	DATE CHANGED
📞	
NOTES	

VENDOR/WEBSITE	
USER NAME	
PASSWORD/PIN	DATE CHANGED
PASSWORD/PIN	DATE CHANGED
PASSWORD/PIN	DATE CHANGED
📞	
NOTES	

G

VENDOR/WEBSITE	
USER NAME	
PASSWORD/PIN	DATE CHANGED
PASSWORD/PIN	DATE CHANGED
PASSWORD/PIN	DATE CHANGED
📞	
NOTES	

VENDOR/WEBSITE	
USER NAME	
PASSWORD/PIN	DATE CHANGED
PASSWORD/PIN	DATE CHANGED
PASSWORD/PIN	DATE CHANGED
📞	
NOTES	

VENDOR/WEBSITE	
USER NAME	
PASSWORD/PIN	DATE CHANGED
PASSWORD/PIN	DATE CHANGED
PASSWORD/PIN	DATE CHANGED
📞	
NOTES	

VENDOR/WEBSITE	
USER NAME	
PASSWORD/PIN	DATE CHANGED
PASSWORD/PIN	DATE CHANGED
PASSWORD/PIN	DATE CHANGED
📞	
NOTES	

	G
VENDOR/WEBSITE	
USER NAME	
PASSWORD/PIN	DATE CHANGED
PASSWORD/PIN	DATE CHANGED
PASSWORD/PIN	DATE CHANGED
📞	
NOTES	
VENDOR/WEBSITE	
USER NAME	
PASSWORD/PIN	DATE CHANGED
PASSWORD/PIN	DATE CHANGED
PASSWORD/PIN	DATE CHANGED
📞	
NOTES	
VENDOR/WEBSITE	
USER NAME	
PASSWORD/PIN	DATE CHANGED
PASSWORD/PIN	DATE CHANGED
PASSWORD/PIN	DATE CHANGED
📞	
NOTES	
VENDOR/WEBSITE	
USER NAME	
PASSWORD/PIN	DATE CHANGED
PASSWORD/PIN	DATE CHANGED
PASSWORD/PIN	DATE CHANGED
📞	
NOTES	

H

VENDOR/WEBSITE	
USER NAME	
PASSWORD/PIN	DATE CHANGED
PASSWORD/PIN	DATE CHANGED
PASSWORD/PIN	DATE CHANGED
📞	
NOTES	

VENDOR/WEBSITE	
USER NAME	
PASSWORD/PIN	DATE CHANGED
PASSWORD/PIN	DATE CHANGED
PASSWORD/PIN	DATE CHANGED
📞	
NOTES	

VENDOR/WEBSITE	
USER NAME	
PASSWORD/PIN	DATE CHANGED
PASSWORD/PIN	DATE CHANGED
PASSWORD/PIN	DATE CHANGED
📞	
NOTES	

VENDOR/WEBSITE	
USER NAME	
PASSWORD/PIN	DATE CHANGED
PASSWORD/PIN	DATE CHANGED
PASSWORD/PIN	DATE CHANGED
📞	
NOTES	

VENDOR/WEBSITE	
USER NAME	
PASSWORD/PIN	DATE CHANGED
PASSWORD/PIN	DATE CHANGED
PASSWORD/PIN	DATE CHANGED
📞	
NOTES	

VENDOR/WEBSITE	
USER NAME	
PASSWORD/PIN	DATE CHANGED
PASSWORD/PIN	DATE CHANGED
PASSWORD/PIN	DATE CHANGED
📞	
NOTES	

VENDOR/WEBSITE	
USER NAME	
PASSWORD/PIN	DATE CHANGED
PASSWORD/PIN	DATE CHANGED
PASSWORD/PIN	DATE CHANGED
📞	
NOTES	

VENDOR/WEBSITE	
USER NAME	
PASSWORD/PIN	DATE CHANGED
PASSWORD/PIN	DATE CHANGED
PASSWORD/PIN	DATE CHANGED
📞	
NOTES	

H

VENDOR/WEBSITE	
USER NAME	
PASSWORD/PIN	DATE CHANGED
PASSWORD/PIN	DATE CHANGED
PASSWORD/PIN	DATE CHANGED
📞	
NOTES	

VENDOR/WEBSITE	
USER NAME	
PASSWORD/PIN	DATE CHANGED
PASSWORD/PIN	DATE CHANGED
PASSWORD/PIN	DATE CHANGED
📞	
NOTES	

VENDOR/WEBSITE	
USER NAME	
PASSWORD/PIN	DATE CHANGED
PASSWORD/PIN	DATE CHANGED
PASSWORD/PIN	DATE CHANGED
📞	
NOTES	

VENDOR/WEBSITE	
USER NAME	
PASSWORD/PIN	DATE CHANGED
PASSWORD/PIN	DATE CHANGED
PASSWORD/PIN	DATE CHANGED
📞	
NOTES	

	H
VENDOR/WEBSITE	
USER NAME	
PASSWORD/PIN	DATE CHANGED
PASSWORD/PIN	DATE CHANGED
PASSWORD/PIN	DATE CHANGED
📞	
NOTES	
VENDOR/WEBSITE	
USER NAME	
PASSWORD/PIN	DATE CHANGED
PASSWORD/PIN	DATE CHANGED
PASSWORD/PIN	DATE CHANGED
📞	
NOTES	
VENDOR/WEBSITE	
USER NAME	
PASSWORD/PIN	DATE CHANGED
PASSWORD/PIN	DATE CHANGED
PASSWORD/PIN	DATE CHANGED
📞	
NOTES	
VENDOR/WEBSITE	
USER NAME	
PASSWORD/PIN	DATE CHANGED
PASSWORD/PIN	DATE CHANGED
PASSWORD/PIN	DATE CHANGED
📞	
NOTES	

I	
VENDOR/WEBSITE	
USER NAME	
PASSWORD/PIN	DATE CHANGED
PASSWORD/PIN	DATE CHANGED
PASSWORD/PIN	DATE CHANGED
☎	
NOTES	
VENDOR/WEBSITE	
USER NAME	
PASSWORD/PIN	DATE CHANGED
PASSWORD/PIN	DATE CHANGED
PASSWORD/PIN	DATE CHANGED
☎	
NOTES	
VENDOR/WEBSITE	
USER NAME	
PASSWORD/PIN	DATE CHANGED
PASSWORD/PIN	DATE CHANGED
PASSWORD/PIN	DATE CHANGED
☎	
NOTES	
VENDOR/WEBSITE	
USER NAME	
PASSWORD/PIN	DATE CHANGED
PASSWORD/PIN	DATE CHANGED
PASSWORD/PIN	DATE CHANGED
☎	
NOTES	

VENDOR/WEBSITE	
USER NAME	
PASSWORD/PIN	DATE CHANGED
PASSWORD/PIN	DATE CHANGED
PASSWORD/PIN	DATE CHANGED
☎	
NOTES	
VENDOR/WEBSITE	
USER NAME	
PASSWORD/PIN	DATE CHANGED
PASSWORD/PIN	DATE CHANGED
PASSWORD/PIN	DATE CHANGED
☎	
NOTES	
VENDOR/WEBSITE	
USER NAME	
PASSWORD/PIN	DATE CHANGED
PASSWORD/PIN	DATE CHANGED
PASSWORD/PIN	DATE CHANGED
☎	
NOTES	
VENDOR/WEBSITE	
USER NAME	
PASSWORD/PIN	DATE CHANGED
PASSWORD/PIN	DATE CHANGED
PASSWORD/PIN	DATE CHANGED
☎	
NOTES	

VENDOR/WEBSITE
USER NAME
PASSWORD/PIN   DATE CHANGED
PASSWORD/PIN   DATE CHANGED
PASSWORD/PIN   DATE CHANGED
☏
NOTES
VENDOR/WEBSITE
USER NAME
PASSWORD/PIN   DATE CHANGED
PASSWORD/PIN   DATE CHANGED
PASSWORD/PIN   DATE CHANGED
☏
NOTES
VENDOR/WEBSITE
USER NAME
PASSWORD/PIN   DATE CHANGED
PASSWORD/PIN   DATE CHANGED
PASSWORD/PIN   DATE CHANGED
☏
NOTES
VENDOR/WEBSITE
USER NAME
PASSWORD/PIN   DATE CHANGED
PASSWORD/PIN   DATE CHANGED
PASSWORD/PIN   DATE CHANGED
☏
NOTES

VENDOR/WEBSITE	
USER NAME	
PASSWORD/PIN	DATE CHANGED
PASSWORD/PIN	DATE CHANGED
PASSWORD/PIN	DATE CHANGED
📞	
NOTES	
VENDOR/WEBSITE	
USER NAME	
PASSWORD/PIN	DATE CHANGED
PASSWORD/PIN	DATE CHANGED
PASSWORD/PIN	DATE CHANGED
📞	
NOTES	
VENDOR/WEBSITE	
USER NAME	
PASSWORD/PIN	DATE CHANGED
PASSWORD/PIN	DATE CHANGED
PASSWORD/PIN	DATE CHANGED
📞	
NOTES	
VENDOR/WEBSITE	
USER NAME	
PASSWORD/PIN	DATE CHANGED
PASSWORD/PIN	DATE CHANGED
PASSWORD/PIN	DATE CHANGED
📞	
NOTES	

J

VENDOR/WEBSITE	
USER NAME	
PASSWORD/PIN	DATE CHANGED
PASSWORD/PIN	DATE CHANGED
PASSWORD/PIN	DATE CHANGED
📞	
NOTES	

VENDOR/WEBSITE	
USER NAME	
PASSWORD/PIN	DATE CHANGED
PASSWORD/PIN	DATE CHANGED
PASSWORD/PIN	DATE CHANGED
📞	
NOTES	

VENDOR/WEBSITE	
USER NAME	
PASSWORD/PIN	DATE CHANGED
PASSWORD/PIN	DATE CHANGED
PASSWORD/PIN	DATE CHANGED
📞	
NOTES	

VENDOR/WEBSITE	
USER NAME	
PASSWORD/PIN	DATE CHANGED
PASSWORD/PIN	DATE CHANGED
PASSWORD/PIN	DATE CHANGED
📞	
NOTES	

	J

VENDOR/WEBSITE	
USER NAME	
PASSWORD/PIN	DATE CHANGED
PASSWORD/PIN	DATE CHANGED
PASSWORD/PIN	DATE CHANGED
📞	
NOTES	

VENDOR/WEBSITE	
USER NAME	
PASSWORD/PIN	DATE CHANGED
PASSWORD/PIN	DATE CHANGED
PASSWORD/PIN	DATE CHANGED
📞	
NOTES	

VENDOR/WEBSITE	
USER NAME	
PASSWORD/PIN	DATE CHANGED
PASSWORD/PIN	DATE CHANGED
PASSWORD/PIN	DATE CHANGED
📞	
NOTES	

VENDOR/WEBSITE	
USER NAME	
PASSWORD/PIN	DATE CHANGED
PASSWORD/PIN	DATE CHANGED
PASSWORD/PIN	DATE CHANGED
📞	
NOTES	

J

VENDOR/WEBSITE	
USER NAME	
PASSWORD/PIN	DATE CHANGED
PASSWORD/PIN	DATE CHANGED
PASSWORD/PIN	DATE CHANGED
☎	
NOTES	

VENDOR/WEBSITE	
USER NAME	
PASSWORD/PIN	DATE CHANGED
PASSWORD/PIN	DATE CHANGED
PASSWORD/PIN	DATE CHANGED
☎	
NOTES	

VENDOR/WEBSITE	
USER NAME	
PASSWORD/PIN	DATE CHANGED
PASSWORD/PIN	DATE CHANGED
PASSWORD/PIN	DATE CHANGED
☎	
NOTES	

VENDOR/WEBSITE	
USER NAME	
PASSWORD/PIN	DATE CHANGED
PASSWORD/PIN	DATE CHANGED
PASSWORD/PIN	DATE CHANGED
☎	
NOTES	

VENDOR/WEBSITE	
USER NAME	
PASSWORD/PIN	DATE CHANGED
PASSWORD/PIN	DATE CHANGED
PASSWORD/PIN	DATE CHANGED
NOTES	

VENDOR/WEBSITE	
USER NAME	
PASSWORD/PIN	DATE CHANGED
PASSWORD/PIN	DATE CHANGED
PASSWORD/PIN	DATE CHANGED
NOTES	

VENDOR/WEBSITE	
USER NAME	
PASSWORD/PIN	DATE CHANGED
PASSWORD/PIN	DATE CHANGED
PASSWORD/PIN	DATE CHANGED
NOTES	

VENDOR/WEBSITE	
USER NAME	
PASSWORD/PIN	DATE CHANGED
PASSWORD/PIN	DATE CHANGED
PASSWORD/PIN	DATE CHANGED
NOTES	

K

VENDOR/WEBSITE	
USER NAME	
PASSWORD/PIN	DATE CHANGED
PASSWORD/PIN	DATE CHANGED
PASSWORD/PIN	DATE CHANGED
☎	
NOTES	

VENDOR/WEBSITE	
USER NAME	
PASSWORD/PIN	DATE CHANGED
PASSWORD/PIN	DATE CHANGED
PASSWORD/PIN	DATE CHANGED
☎	
NOTES	

VENDOR/WEBSITE	
USER NAME	
PASSWORD/PIN	DATE CHANGED
PASSWORD/PIN	DATE CHANGED
PASSWORD/PIN	DATE CHANGED
☎	
NOTES	

VENDOR/WEBSITE	
USER NAME	
PASSWORD/PIN	DATE CHANGED
PASSWORD/PIN	DATE CHANGED
PASSWORD/PIN	DATE CHANGED
☎	
NOTES	

VENDOR/WEBSITE	
USER NAME	
PASSWORD/PIN	DATE CHANGED
PASSWORD/PIN	DATE CHANGED
PASSWORD/PIN	DATE CHANGED
☎	
NOTES	
VENDOR/WEBSITE	
USER NAME	
PASSWORD/PIN	DATE CHANGED
PASSWORD/PIN	DATE CHANGED
PASSWORD/PIN	DATE CHANGED
☎	
NOTES	
VENDOR/WEBSITE	
USER NAME	
PASSWORD/PIN	DATE CHANGED
PASSWORD/PIN	DATE CHANGED
PASSWORD/PIN	DATE CHANGED
☎	
NOTES	
VENDOR/WEBSITE	
USER NAME	
PASSWORD/PIN	DATE CHANGED
PASSWORD/PIN	DATE CHANGED
PASSWORD/PIN	DATE CHANGED
☎	
NOTES	

K

VENDOR/WEBSITE	
USER NAME	
PASSWORD/PIN	DATE CHANGED
PASSWORD/PIN	DATE CHANGED
PASSWORD/PIN	DATE CHANGED
📞	
NOTES	

VENDOR/WEBSITE	
USER NAME	
PASSWORD/PIN	DATE CHANGED
PASSWORD/PIN	DATE CHANGED
PASSWORD/PIN	DATE CHANGED
📞	
NOTES	

VENDOR/WEBSITE	
USER NAME	
PASSWORD/PIN	DATE CHANGED
PASSWORD/PIN	DATE CHANGED
PASSWORD/PIN	DATE CHANGED
📞	
NOTES	

VENDOR/WEBSITE	
USER NAME	
PASSWORD/PIN	DATE CHANGED
PASSWORD/PIN	DATE CHANGED
PASSWORD/PIN	DATE CHANGED
📞	
NOTES	

	K
VENDOR/WEBSITE	
USER NAME	
PASSWORD/PIN	DATE CHANGED
PASSWORD/PIN	DATE CHANGED
PASSWORD/PIN	DATE CHANGED
☎	
NOTES	
VENDOR/WEBSITE	
USER NAME	
PASSWORD/PIN	DATE CHANGED
PASSWORD/PIN	DATE CHANGED
PASSWORD/PIN	DATE CHANGED
☎	
NOTES	
VENDOR/WEBSITE	
USER NAME	
PASSWORD/PIN	DATE CHANGED
PASSWORD/PIN	DATE CHANGED
PASSWORD/PIN	DATE CHANGED
☎	
NOTES	
VENDOR/WEBSITE	
USER NAME	
PASSWORD/PIN	DATE CHANGED
PASSWORD/PIN	DATE CHANGED
PASSWORD/PIN	DATE CHANGED
☎	
NOTES	

L

VENDOR/WEBSITE	
USER NAME	
PASSWORD/PIN	DATE CHANGED
PASSWORD/PIN	DATE CHANGED
PASSWORD/PIN	DATE CHANGED
📞	
NOTES	

VENDOR/WEBSITE	
USER NAME	
PASSWORD/PIN	DATE CHANGED
PASSWORD/PIN	DATE CHANGED
PASSWORD/PIN	DATE CHANGED
📞	
NOTES	

VENDOR/WEBSITE	
USER NAME	
PASSWORD/PIN	DATE CHANGED
PASSWORD/PIN	DATE CHANGED
PASSWORD/PIN	DATE CHANGED
📞	
NOTES	

VENDOR/WEBSITE	
USER NAME	
PASSWORD/PIN	DATE CHANGED
PASSWORD/PIN	DATE CHANGED
PASSWORD/PIN	DATE CHANGED
📞	
NOTES	

	L
VENDOR/WEBSITE	
USER NAME	
PASSWORD/PIN	DATE CHANGED
PASSWORD/PIN	DATE CHANGED
PASSWORD/PIN	DATE CHANGED
NOTES	
VENDOR/WEBSITE	
USER NAME	
PASSWORD/PIN	DATE CHANGED
PASSWORD/PIN	DATE CHANGED
PASSWORD/PIN	DATE CHANGED
NOTES	
VENDOR/WEBSITE	
USER NAME	
PASSWORD/PIN	DATE CHANGED
PASSWORD/PIN	DATE CHANGED
PASSWORD/PIN	DATE CHANGED
NOTES	
VENDOR/WEBSITE	
USER NAME	
PASSWORD/PIN	DATE CHANGED
PASSWORD/PIN	DATE CHANGED
PASSWORD/PIN	DATE CHANGED
NOTES	

L

VENDOR/WEBSITE	
USER NAME	
PASSWORD/PIN	DATE CHANGED
PASSWORD/PIN	DATE CHANGED
PASSWORD/PIN	DATE CHANGED
📞	
NOTES	

VENDOR/WEBSITE	
USER NAME	
PASSWORD/PIN	DATE CHANGED
PASSWORD/PIN	DATE CHANGED
PASSWORD/PIN	DATE CHANGED
📞	
NOTES	

VENDOR/WEBSITE	
USER NAME	
PASSWORD/PIN	DATE CHANGED
PASSWORD/PIN	DATE CHANGED
PASSWORD/PIN	DATE CHANGED
📞	
NOTES	

VENDOR/WEBSITE	
USER NAME	
PASSWORD/PIN	DATE CHANGED
PASSWORD/PIN	DATE CHANGED
PASSWORD/PIN	DATE CHANGED
📞	
NOTES	

	L
VENDOR/WEBSITE	
USER NAME	
PASSWORD/PIN	DATE CHANGED
PASSWORD/PIN	DATE CHANGED
PASSWORD/PIN	DATE CHANGED
📞	
NOTES	
VENDOR/WEBSITE	
USER NAME	
PASSWORD/PIN	DATE CHANGED
PASSWORD/PIN	DATE CHANGED
PASSWORD/PIN	DATE CHANGED
📞	
NOTES	
VENDOR/WEBSITE	
USER NAME	
PASSWORD/PIN	DATE CHANGED
PASSWORD/PIN	DATE CHANGED
PASSWORD/PIN	DATE CHANGED
📞	
NOTES	
VENDOR/WEBSITE	
USER NAME	
PASSWORD/PIN	DATE CHANGED
PASSWORD/PIN	DATE CHANGED
PASSWORD/PIN	DATE CHANGED
📞	
NOTES	

M

VENDOR/WEBSITE	
USER NAME	
PASSWORD/PIN	DATE CHANGED
PASSWORD/PIN	DATE CHANGED
PASSWORD/PIN	DATE CHANGED
📞	
NOTES	

VENDOR/WEBSITE	
USER NAME	
PASSWORD/PIN	DATE CHANGED
PASSWORD/PIN	DATE CHANGED
PASSWORD/PIN	DATE CHANGED
📞	
NOTES	

VENDOR/WEBSITE	
USER NAME	
PASSWORD/PIN	DATE CHANGED
PASSWORD/PIN	DATE CHANGED
PASSWORD/PIN	DATE CHANGED
📞	
NOTES	

VENDOR/WEBSITE	
USER NAME	
PASSWORD/PIN	DATE CHANGED
PASSWORD/PIN	DATE CHANGED
PASSWORD/PIN	DATE CHANGED
📞	
NOTES	

M

VENDOR/WEBSITE	
USER NAME	
PASSWORD/PIN	DATE CHANGED
PASSWORD/PIN	DATE CHANGED
PASSWORD/PIN	DATE CHANGED
📞	
NOTES	

VENDOR/WEBSITE	
USER NAME	
PASSWORD/PIN	DATE CHANGED
PASSWORD/PIN	DATE CHANGED
PASSWORD/PIN	DATE CHANGED
📞	
NOTES	

VENDOR/WEBSITE	
USER NAME	
PASSWORD/PIN	DATE CHANGED
PASSWORD/PIN	DATE CHANGED
PASSWORD/PIN	DATE CHANGED
📞	
NOTES	

VENDOR/WEBSITE	
USER NAME	
PASSWORD/PIN	DATE CHANGED
PASSWORD/PIN	DATE CHANGED
PASSWORD/PIN	DATE CHANGED
📞	
NOTES	

M

VENDOR/WEBSITE	
USER NAME	
PASSWORD/PIN	DATE CHANGED
PASSWORD/PIN	DATE CHANGED
PASSWORD/PIN	DATE CHANGED
☎	
NOTES	

VENDOR/WEBSITE	
USER NAME	
PASSWORD/PIN	DATE CHANGED
PASSWORD/PIN	DATE CHANGED
PASSWORD/PIN	DATE CHANGED
☎	
NOTES	

VENDOR/WEBSITE	
USER NAME	
PASSWORD/PIN	DATE CHANGED
PASSWORD/PIN	DATE CHANGED
PASSWORD/PIN	DATE CHANGED
☎	
NOTES	

VENDOR/WEBSITE	
USER NAME	
PASSWORD/PIN	DATE CHANGED
PASSWORD/PIN	DATE CHANGED
PASSWORD/PIN	DATE CHANGED
☎	
NOTES	

VENDOR/WEBSITE	
USER NAME	
PASSWORD/PIN	DATE CHANGED
PASSWORD/PIN	DATE CHANGED
PASSWORD/PIN	DATE CHANGED
☎	
NOTES	

VENDOR/WEBSITE	
USER NAME	
PASSWORD/PIN	DATE CHANGED
PASSWORD/PIN	DATE CHANGED
PASSWORD/PIN	DATE CHANGED
☎	
NOTES	

VENDOR/WEBSITE	
USER NAME	
PASSWORD/PIN	DATE CHANGED
PASSWORD/PIN	DATE CHANGED
PASSWORD/PIN	DATE CHANGED
☎	
NOTES	

VENDOR/WEBSITE	
USER NAME	
PASSWORD/PIN	DATE CHANGED
PASSWORD/PIN	DATE CHANGED
PASSWORD/PIN	DATE CHANGED
☎	
NOTES	

N

VENDOR/WEBSITE	
USER NAME	
PASSWORD/PIN	DATE CHANGED
PASSWORD/PIN	DATE CHANGED
PASSWORD/PIN	DATE CHANGED
📞	
NOTES	

VENDOR/WEBSITE	
USER NAME	
PASSWORD/PIN	DATE CHANGED
PASSWORD/PIN	DATE CHANGED
PASSWORD/PIN	DATE CHANGED
📞	
NOTES	

VENDOR/WEBSITE	
USER NAME	
PASSWORD/PIN	DATE CHANGED
PASSWORD/PIN	DATE CHANGED
PASSWORD/PIN	DATE CHANGED
📞	
NOTES	

VENDOR/WEBSITE	
USER NAME	
PASSWORD/PIN	DATE CHANGED
PASSWORD/PIN	DATE CHANGED
PASSWORD/PIN	DATE CHANGED
📞	
NOTES	

VENDOR/WEBSITE	
USER NAME	
PASSWORD/PIN	DATE CHANGED
PASSWORD/PIN	DATE CHANGED
PASSWORD/PIN	DATE CHANGED
☎	
NOTES	
VENDOR/WEBSITE	
USER NAME	
PASSWORD/PIN	DATE CHANGED
PASSWORD/PIN	DATE CHANGED
PASSWORD/PIN	DATE CHANGED
☎	
NOTES	
VENDOR/WEBSITE	
USER NAME	
PASSWORD/PIN	DATE CHANGED
PASSWORD/PIN	DATE CHANGED
PASSWORD/PIN	DATE CHANGED
☎	
NOTES	
VENDOR/WEBSITE	
USER NAME	
PASSWORD/PIN	DATE CHANGED
PASSWORD/PIN	DATE CHANGED
PASSWORD/PIN	DATE CHANGED
☎	
NOTES	

N

VENDOR/WEBSITE	
USER NAME	
PASSWORD/PIN	DATE CHANGED
PASSWORD/PIN	DATE CHANGED
PASSWORD/PIN	DATE CHANGED
☎	
NOTES	

VENDOR/WEBSITE	
USER NAME	
PASSWORD/PIN	DATE CHANGED
PASSWORD/PIN	DATE CHANGED
PASSWORD/PIN	DATE CHANGED
☎	
NOTES	

VENDOR/WEBSITE	
USER NAME	
PASSWORD/PIN	DATE CHANGED
PASSWORD/PIN	DATE CHANGED
PASSWORD/PIN	DATE CHANGED
☎	
NOTES	

VENDOR/WEBSITE	
USER NAME	
PASSWORD/PIN	DATE CHANGED
PASSWORD/PIN	DATE CHANGED
PASSWORD/PIN	DATE CHANGED
☎	
NOTES	

VENDOR/WEBSITE	
USER NAME	
PASSWORD/PIN	DATE CHANGED
PASSWORD/PIN	DATE CHANGED
PASSWORD/PIN	DATE CHANGED
NOTES	

VENDOR/WEBSITE	
USER NAME	
PASSWORD/PIN	DATE CHANGED
PASSWORD/PIN	DATE CHANGED
PASSWORD/PIN	DATE CHANGED
NOTES	

VENDOR/WEBSITE	
USER NAME	
PASSWORD/PIN	DATE CHANGED
PASSWORD/PIN	DATE CHANGED
PASSWORD/PIN	DATE CHANGED
NOTES	

VENDOR/WEBSITE	
USER NAME	
PASSWORD/PIN	DATE CHANGED
PASSWORD/PIN	DATE CHANGED
PASSWORD/PIN	DATE CHANGED
NOTES	

0	
VENDOR/WEBSITE	
USER NAME	
PASSWORD/PIN	DATE CHANGED
PASSWORD/PIN	DATE CHANGED
PASSWORD/PIN	DATE CHANGED
📞	
NOTES	
VENDOR/WEBSITE	
USER NAME	
PASSWORD/PIN	DATE CHANGED
PASSWORD/PIN	DATE CHANGED
PASSWORD/PIN	DATE CHANGED
📞	
NOTES	
VENDOR/WEBSITE	
USER NAME	
PASSWORD/PIN	DATE CHANGED
PASSWORD/PIN	DATE CHANGED
PASSWORD/PIN	DATE CHANGED
📞	
NOTES	
VENDOR/WEBSITE	
USER NAME	
PASSWORD/PIN	DATE CHANGED
PASSWORD/PIN	DATE CHANGED
PASSWORD/PIN	DATE CHANGED
📞	
NOTES	

	0
VENDOR/WEBSITE	
USER NAME	
PASSWORD/PIN	DATE CHANGED
PASSWORD/PIN	DATE CHANGED
PASSWORD/PIN	DATE CHANGED
☎	
NOTES	
VENDOR/WEBSITE	
USER NAME	
PASSWORD/PIN	DATE CHANGED
PASSWORD/PIN	DATE CHANGED
PASSWORD/PIN	DATE CHANGED
☎	
NOTES	
VENDOR/WEBSITE	
USER NAME	
PASSWORD/PIN	DATE CHANGED
PASSWORD/PIN	DATE CHANGED
PASSWORD/PIN	DATE CHANGED
☎	
NOTES	
VENDOR/WEBSITE	
USER NAME	
PASSWORD/PIN	DATE CHANGED
PASSWORD/PIN	DATE CHANGED
PASSWORD/PIN	DATE CHANGED
☎	
NOTES	

0	
VENDOR/WEBSITE	
USER NAME	
PASSWORD/PIN	DATE CHANGED
PASSWORD/PIN	DATE CHANGED
PASSWORD/PIN	DATE CHANGED
📞	
NOTES	
VENDOR/WEBSITE	
USER NAME	
PASSWORD/PIN	DATE CHANGED
PASSWORD/PIN	DATE CHANGED
PASSWORD/PIN	DATE CHANGED
📞	
NOTES	
VENDOR/WEBSITE	
USER NAME	
PASSWORD/PIN	DATE CHANGED
PASSWORD/PIN	DATE CHANGED
PASSWORD/PIN	DATE CHANGED
📞	
NOTES	
VENDOR/WEBSITE	
USER NAME	
PASSWORD/PIN	DATE CHANGED
PASSWORD/PIN	DATE CHANGED
PASSWORD/PIN	DATE CHANGED
📞	
NOTES	

	0
VENDOR/WEBSITE	
USER NAME	
PASSWORD/PIN	DATE CHANGED
PASSWORD/PIN	DATE CHANGED
PASSWORD/PIN	DATE CHANGED
NOTES	
VENDOR/WEBSITE	
USER NAME	
PASSWORD/PIN	DATE CHANGED
PASSWORD/PIN	DATE CHANGED
PASSWORD/PIN	DATE CHANGED
NOTES	
VENDOR/WEBSITE	
USER NAME	
PASSWORD/PIN	DATE CHANGED
PASSWORD/PIN	DATE CHANGED
PASSWORD/PIN	DATE CHANGED
NOTES	
VENDOR/WEBSITE	
USER NAME	
PASSWORD/PIN	DATE CHANGED
PASSWORD/PIN	DATE CHANGED
PASSWORD/PIN	DATE CHANGED
NOTES	

P

VENDOR/WEBSITE	
USER NAME	
PASSWORD/PIN	DATE CHANGED
PASSWORD/PIN	DATE CHANGED
PASSWORD/PIN	DATE CHANGED
☎	
NOTES	

VENDOR/WEBSITE	
USER NAME	
PASSWORD/PIN	DATE CHANGED
PASSWORD/PIN	DATE CHANGED
PASSWORD/PIN	DATE CHANGED
☎	
NOTES	

VENDOR/WEBSITE	
USER NAME	
PASSWORD/PIN	DATE CHANGED
PASSWORD/PIN	DATE CHANGED
PASSWORD/PIN	DATE CHANGED
☎	
NOTES	

VENDOR/WEBSITE	
USER NAME	
PASSWORD/PIN	DATE CHANGED
PASSWORD/PIN	DATE CHANGED
PASSWORD/PIN	DATE CHANGED
☎	
NOTES	

VENDOR/WEBSITE	
USER NAME	
PASSWORD/PIN	DATE CHANGED
PASSWORD/PIN	DATE CHANGED
PASSWORD/PIN	DATE CHANGED
☎	
NOTES	

VENDOR/WEBSITE	
USER NAME	
PASSWORD/PIN	DATE CHANGED
PASSWORD/PIN	DATE CHANGED
PASSWORD/PIN	DATE CHANGED
☎	
NOTES	

VENDOR/WEBSITE	
USER NAME	
PASSWORD/PIN	DATE CHANGED
PASSWORD/PIN	DATE CHANGED
PASSWORD/PIN	DATE CHANGED
☎	
NOTES	

VENDOR/WEBSITE	
USER NAME	
PASSWORD/PIN	DATE CHANGED
PASSWORD/PIN	DATE CHANGED
PASSWORD/PIN	DATE CHANGED
☎	
NOTES	

P
VENDOR/WEBSITE
USER NAME

PASSWORD/PIN	DATE CHANGED
PASSWORD/PIN	DATE CHANGED
PASSWORD/PIN	DATE CHANGED

☎
NOTES

VENDOR/WEBSITE
USER NAME

PASSWORD/PIN	DATE CHANGED
PASSWORD/PIN	DATE CHANGED
PASSWORD/PIN	DATE CHANGED

☎
NOTES

VENDOR/WEBSITE
USER NAME

PASSWORD/PIN	DATE CHANGED
PASSWORD/PIN	DATE CHANGED
PASSWORD/PIN	DATE CHANGED

☎
NOTES

VENDOR/WEBSITE
USER NAME

PASSWORD/PIN	DATE CHANGED
PASSWORD/PIN	DATE CHANGED
PASSWORD/PIN	DATE CHANGED

☎
NOTES

VENDOR/WEBSITE	
USER NAME	
PASSWORD/PIN	DATE CHANGED
PASSWORD/PIN	DATE CHANGED
PASSWORD/PIN	DATE CHANGED
NOTES	

VENDOR/WEBSITE	
USER NAME	
PASSWORD/PIN	DATE CHANGED
PASSWORD/PIN	DATE CHANGED
PASSWORD/PIN	DATE CHANGED
NOTES	

VENDOR/WEBSITE	
USER NAME	
PASSWORD/PIN	DATE CHANGED
PASSWORD/PIN	DATE CHANGED
PASSWORD/PIN	DATE CHANGED
NOTES	

VENDOR/WEBSITE	
USER NAME	
PASSWORD/PIN	DATE CHANGED
PASSWORD/PIN	DATE CHANGED
PASSWORD/PIN	DATE CHANGED
NOTES	

Q

VENDOR/WEBSITE	
USER NAME	
PASSWORD/PIN	DATE CHANGED
PASSWORD/PIN	DATE CHANGED
PASSWORD/PIN	DATE CHANGED
📞	
NOTES	

VENDOR/WEBSITE	
USER NAME	
PASSWORD/PIN	DATE CHANGED
PASSWORD/PIN	DATE CHANGED
PASSWORD/PIN	DATE CHANGED
📞	
NOTES	

VENDOR/WEBSITE	
USER NAME	
PASSWORD/PIN	DATE CHANGED
PASSWORD/PIN	DATE CHANGED
PASSWORD/PIN	DATE CHANGED
📞	
NOTES	

VENDOR/WEBSITE	
USER NAME	
PASSWORD/PIN	DATE CHANGED
PASSWORD/PIN	DATE CHANGED
PASSWORD/PIN	DATE CHANGED
📞	
NOTES	

	Q
VENDOR/WEBSITE	
USER NAME	
PASSWORD/PIN	DATE CHANGED
PASSWORD/PIN	DATE CHANGED
PASSWORD/PIN	DATE CHANGED
☎	
NOTES	
VENDOR/WEBSITE	
USER NAME	
PASSWORD/PIN	DATE CHANGED
PASSWORD/PIN	DATE CHANGED
PASSWORD/PIN	DATE CHANGED
☎	
NOTES	
VENDOR/WEBSITE	
USER NAME	
PASSWORD/PIN	DATE CHANGED
PASSWORD/PIN	DATE CHANGED
PASSWORD/PIN	DATE CHANGED
☎	
NOTES	
VENDOR/WEBSITE	
USER NAME	
PASSWORD/PIN	DATE CHANGED
PASSWORD/PIN	DATE CHANGED
PASSWORD/PIN	DATE CHANGED
☎	
NOTES	

Q

VENDOR/WEBSITE	
USER NAME	
PASSWORD/PIN	DATE CHANGED
PASSWORD/PIN	DATE CHANGED
PASSWORD/PIN	DATE CHANGED
📞	
NOTES	

VENDOR/WEBSITE	
USER NAME	
PASSWORD/PIN	DATE CHANGED
PASSWORD/PIN	DATE CHANGED
PASSWORD/PIN	DATE CHANGED
📞	
NOTES	

VENDOR/WEBSITE	
USER NAME	
PASSWORD/PIN	DATE CHANGED
PASSWORD/PIN	DATE CHANGED
PASSWORD/PIN	DATE CHANGED
📞	
NOTES	

VENDOR/WEBSITE	
USER NAME	
PASSWORD/PIN	DATE CHANGED
PASSWORD/PIN	DATE CHANGED
PASSWORD/PIN	DATE CHANGED
📞	
NOTES	

	Q

VENDOR/WEBSITE	
USER NAME	

PASSWORD/PIN	DATE CHANGED
PASSWORD/PIN	DATE CHANGED
PASSWORD/PIN	DATE CHANGED

NOTES	

VENDOR/WEBSITE	
USER NAME	

PASSWORD/PIN	DATE CHANGED
PASSWORD/PIN	DATE CHANGED
PASSWORD/PIN	DATE CHANGED

NOTES	

VENDOR/WEBSITE	
USER NAME	

PASSWORD/PIN	DATE CHANGED
PASSWORD/PIN	DATE CHANGED
PASSWORD/PIN	DATE CHANGED

NOTES	

VENDOR/WEBSITE	
USER NAME	

PASSWORD/PIN	DATE CHANGED
PASSWORD/PIN	DATE CHANGED
PASSWORD/PIN	DATE CHANGED

NOTES	

R

VENDOR/WEBSITE	
USER NAME	
PASSWORD/PIN	DATE CHANGED
PASSWORD/PIN	DATE CHANGED
PASSWORD/PIN	DATE CHANGED
📞	
NOTES	

VENDOR/WEBSITE	
USER NAME	
PASSWORD/PIN	DATE CHANGED
PASSWORD/PIN	DATE CHANGED
PASSWORD/PIN	DATE CHANGED
📞	
NOTES	

VENDOR/WEBSITE	
USER NAME	
PASSWORD/PIN	DATE CHANGED
PASSWORD/PIN	DATE CHANGED
PASSWORD/PIN	DATE CHANGED
📞	
NOTES	

VENDOR/WEBSITE	
USER NAME	
PASSWORD/PIN	DATE CHANGED
PASSWORD/PIN	DATE CHANGED
PASSWORD/PIN	DATE CHANGED
📞	
NOTES	

	R
VENDOR/WEBSITE	
USER NAME	
PASSWORD/PIN	DATE CHANGED
PASSWORD/PIN	DATE CHANGED
PASSWORD/PIN	DATE CHANGED
NOTES	
VENDOR/WEBSITE	
USER NAME	
PASSWORD/PIN	DATE CHANGED
PASSWORD/PIN	DATE CHANGED
PASSWORD/PIN	DATE CHANGED
NOTES	
VENDOR/WEBSITE	
USER NAME	
PASSWORD/PIN	DATE CHANGED
PASSWORD/PIN	DATE CHANGED
PASSWORD/PIN	DATE CHANGED
NOTES	
VENDOR/WEBSITE	
USER NAME	
PASSWORD/PIN	DATE CHANGED
PASSWORD/PIN	DATE CHANGED
PASSWORD/PIN	DATE CHANGED
NOTES	

R

VENDOR/WEBSITE	
USER NAME	
PASSWORD/PIN	DATE CHANGED
PASSWORD/PIN	DATE CHANGED
PASSWORD/PIN	DATE CHANGED
☎	
NOTES	

VENDOR/WEBSITE	
USER NAME	
PASSWORD/PIN	DATE CHANGED
PASSWORD/PIN	DATE CHANGED
PASSWORD/PIN	DATE CHANGED
☎	
NOTES	

VENDOR/WEBSITE	
USER NAME	
PASSWORD/PIN	DATE CHANGED
PASSWORD/PIN	DATE CHANGED
PASSWORD/PIN	DATE CHANGED
☎	
NOTES	

VENDOR/WEBSITE	
USER NAME	
PASSWORD/PIN	DATE CHANGED
PASSWORD/PIN	DATE CHANGED
PASSWORD/PIN	DATE CHANGED
☎	
NOTES	

	R
VENDOR/WEBSITE	
USER NAME	
PASSWORD/PIN	DATE CHANGED
PASSWORD/PIN	DATE CHANGED
PASSWORD/PIN	DATE CHANGED
☎	
NOTES	
VENDOR/WEBSITE	
USER NAME	
PASSWORD/PIN	DATE CHANGED
PASSWORD/PIN	DATE CHANGED
PASSWORD/PIN	DATE CHANGED
☎	
NOTES	
VENDOR/WEBSITE	
USER NAME	
PASSWORD/PIN	DATE CHANGED
PASSWORD/PIN	DATE CHANGED
PASSWORD/PIN	DATE CHANGED
☎	
NOTES	
VENDOR/WEBSITE	
USER NAME	
PASSWORD/PIN	DATE CHANGED
PASSWORD/PIN	DATE CHANGED
PASSWORD/PIN	DATE CHANGED
☎	
NOTES	

S

VENDOR/WEBSITE	
USER NAME	
PASSWORD/PIN	DATE CHANGED
PASSWORD/PIN	DATE CHANGED
PASSWORD/PIN	DATE CHANGED
📞	
NOTES	

VENDOR/WEBSITE	
USER NAME	
PASSWORD/PIN	DATE CHANGED
PASSWORD/PIN	DATE CHANGED
PASSWORD/PIN	DATE CHANGED
📞	
NOTES	

VENDOR/WEBSITE	
USER NAME	
PASSWORD/PIN	DATE CHANGED
PASSWORD/PIN	DATE CHANGED
PASSWORD/PIN	DATE CHANGED
📞	
NOTES	

VENDOR/WEBSITE	
USER NAME	
PASSWORD/PIN	DATE CHANGED
PASSWORD/PIN	DATE CHANGED
PASSWORD/PIN	DATE CHANGED
📞	
NOTES	

VENDOR/WEBSITE	
USER NAME	
PASSWORD/PIN	DATE CHANGED
PASSWORD/PIN	DATE CHANGED
PASSWORD/PIN	DATE CHANGED
☏	
NOTES	

VENDOR/WEBSITE	
USER NAME	
PASSWORD/PIN	DATE CHANGED
PASSWORD/PIN	DATE CHANGED
PASSWORD/PIN	DATE CHANGED
☏	
NOTES	

VENDOR/WEBSITE	
USER NAME	
PASSWORD/PIN	DATE CHANGED
PASSWORD/PIN	DATE CHANGED
PASSWORD/PIN	DATE CHANGED
☏	
NOTES	

VENDOR/WEBSITE	
USER NAME	
PASSWORD/PIN	DATE CHANGED
PASSWORD/PIN	DATE CHANGED
PASSWORD/PIN	DATE CHANGED
☏	
NOTES	

S

VENDOR/WEBSITE	
USER NAME	
PASSWORD/PIN	DATE CHANGED
PASSWORD/PIN	DATE CHANGED
PASSWORD/PIN	DATE CHANGED
📞	
NOTES	

VENDOR/WEBSITE	
USER NAME	
PASSWORD/PIN	DATE CHANGED
PASSWORD/PIN	DATE CHANGED
PASSWORD/PIN	DATE CHANGED
📞	
NOTES	

VENDOR/WEBSITE	
USER NAME	
PASSWORD/PIN	DATE CHANGED
PASSWORD/PIN	DATE CHANGED
PASSWORD/PIN	DATE CHANGED
📞	
NOTES	

VENDOR/WEBSITE	
USER NAME	
PASSWORD/PIN	DATE CHANGED
PASSWORD/PIN	DATE CHANGED
PASSWORD/PIN	DATE CHANGED
📞	
NOTES	

VENDOR/WEBSITE	
USER NAME	
PASSWORD/PIN	DATE CHANGED
PASSWORD/PIN	DATE CHANGED
PASSWORD/PIN	DATE CHANGED
📞	
NOTES	

VENDOR/WEBSITE	
USER NAME	
PASSWORD/PIN	DATE CHANGED
PASSWORD/PIN	DATE CHANGED
PASSWORD/PIN	DATE CHANGED
📞	
NOTES	

VENDOR/WEBSITE	
USER NAME	
PASSWORD/PIN	DATE CHANGED
PASSWORD/PIN	DATE CHANGED
PASSWORD/PIN	DATE CHANGED
📞	
NOTES	

VENDOR/WEBSITE	
USER NAME	
PASSWORD/PIN	DATE CHANGED
PASSWORD/PIN	DATE CHANGED
PASSWORD/PIN	DATE CHANGED
📞	
NOTES	

T

VENDOR/WEBSITE	
USER NAME	
PASSWORD/PIN	DATE CHANGED
PASSWORD/PIN	DATE CHANGED
PASSWORD/PIN	DATE CHANGED
📞	
NOTES	

VENDOR/WEBSITE	
USER NAME	
PASSWORD/PIN	DATE CHANGED
PASSWORD/PIN	DATE CHANGED
PASSWORD/PIN	DATE CHANGED
📞	
NOTES	

VENDOR/WEBSITE	
USER NAME	
PASSWORD/PIN	DATE CHANGED
PASSWORD/PIN	DATE CHANGED
PASSWORD/PIN	DATE CHANGED
📞	
NOTES	

VENDOR/WEBSITE	
USER NAME	
PASSWORD/PIN	DATE CHANGED
PASSWORD/PIN	DATE CHANGED
PASSWORD/PIN	DATE CHANGED
📞	
NOTES	

	T
VENDOR/WEBSITE	
USER NAME	
PASSWORD/PIN	DATE CHANGED
PASSWORD/PIN	DATE CHANGED
PASSWORD/PIN	DATE CHANGED
📞	
NOTES	
VENDOR/WEBSITE	
USER NAME	
PASSWORD/PIN	DATE CHANGED
PASSWORD/PIN	DATE CHANGED
PASSWORD/PIN	DATE CHANGED
📞	
NOTES	
VENDOR/WEBSITE	
USER NAME	
PASSWORD/PIN	DATE CHANGED
PASSWORD/PIN	DATE CHANGED
PASSWORD/PIN	DATE CHANGED
📞	
NOTES	
VENDOR/WEBSITE	
USER NAME	
PASSWORD/PIN	DATE CHANGED
PASSWORD/PIN	DATE CHANGED
PASSWORD/PIN	DATE CHANGED
📞	
NOTES	

T

VENDOR/WEBSITE	
USER NAME	
PASSWORD/PIN	DATE CHANGED
PASSWORD/PIN	DATE CHANGED
PASSWORD/PIN	DATE CHANGED
📞	
NOTES	

VENDOR/WEBSITE	
USER NAME	
PASSWORD/PIN	DATE CHANGED
PASSWORD/PIN	DATE CHANGED
PASSWORD/PIN	DATE CHANGED
📞	
NOTES	

VENDOR/WEBSITE	
USER NAME	
PASSWORD/PIN	DATE CHANGED
PASSWORD/PIN	DATE CHANGED
PASSWORD/PIN	DATE CHANGED
📞	
NOTES	

VENDOR/WEBSITE	
USER NAME	
PASSWORD/PIN	DATE CHANGED
PASSWORD/PIN	DATE CHANGED
PASSWORD/PIN	DATE CHANGED
📞	
NOTES	

	T
VENDOR/WEBSITE	
USER NAME	
PASSWORD/PIN	DATE CHANGED
PASSWORD/PIN	DATE CHANGED
PASSWORD/PIN	DATE CHANGED
NOTES	
VENDOR/WEBSITE	
USER NAME	
PASSWORD/PIN	DATE CHANGED
PASSWORD/PIN	DATE CHANGED
PASSWORD/PIN	DATE CHANGED
NOTES	
VENDOR/WEBSITE	
USER NAME	
PASSWORD/PIN	DATE CHANGED
PASSWORD/PIN	DATE CHANGED
PASSWORD/PIN	DATE CHANGED
NOTES	
VENDOR/WEBSITE	
USER NAME	
PASSWORD/PIN	DATE CHANGED
PASSWORD/PIN	DATE CHANGED
PASSWORD/PIN	DATE CHANGED
NOTES	

U

VENDOR/WEBSITE	
USER NAME	
PASSWORD/PIN	DATE CHANGED
PASSWORD/PIN	DATE CHANGED
PASSWORD/PIN	DATE CHANGED
📞	
NOTES	

VENDOR/WEBSITE	
USER NAME	
PASSWORD/PIN	DATE CHANGED
PASSWORD/PIN	DATE CHANGED
PASSWORD/PIN	DATE CHANGED
📞	
NOTES	

VENDOR/WEBSITE	
USER NAME	
PASSWORD/PIN	DATE CHANGED
PASSWORD/PIN	DATE CHANGED
PASSWORD/PIN	DATE CHANGED
📞	
NOTES	

VENDOR/WEBSITE	
USER NAME	
PASSWORD/PIN	DATE CHANGED
PASSWORD/PIN	DATE CHANGED
PASSWORD/PIN	DATE CHANGED
📞	
NOTES	

U

VENDOR/WEBSITE	
USER NAME	
PASSWORD/PIN	DATE CHANGED
PASSWORD/PIN	DATE CHANGED
PASSWORD/PIN	DATE CHANGED
📞	
NOTES	

VENDOR/WEBSITE	
USER NAME	
PASSWORD/PIN	DATE CHANGED
PASSWORD/PIN	DATE CHANGED
PASSWORD/PIN	DATE CHANGED
📞	
NOTES	

VENDOR/WEBSITE	
USER NAME	
PASSWORD/PIN	DATE CHANGED
PASSWORD/PIN	DATE CHANGED
PASSWORD/PIN	DATE CHANGED
📞	
NOTES	

VENDOR/WEBSITE	
USER NAME	
PASSWORD/PIN	DATE CHANGED
PASSWORD/PIN	DATE CHANGED
PASSWORD/PIN	DATE CHANGED
📞	
NOTES	

U

VENDOR/WEBSITE	
USER NAME	
PASSWORD/PIN	DATE CHANGED
PASSWORD/PIN	DATE CHANGED
PASSWORD/PIN	DATE CHANGED
📞	
NOTES	
VENDOR/WEBSITE	
USER NAME	
PASSWORD/PIN	DATE CHANGED
PASSWORD/PIN	DATE CHANGED
PASSWORD/PIN	DATE CHANGED
📞	
NOTES	
VENDOR/WEBSITE	
USER NAME	
PASSWORD/PIN	DATE CHANGED
PASSWORD/PIN	DATE CHANGED
PASSWORD/PIN	DATE CHANGED
📞	
NOTES	
VENDOR/WEBSITE	
USER NAME	
PASSWORD/PIN	DATE CHANGED
PASSWORD/PIN	DATE CHANGED
PASSWORD/PIN	DATE CHANGED
📞	
NOTES	

VENDOR/WEBSITE	
USER NAME	
PASSWORD/PIN	DATE CHANGED
PASSWORD/PIN	DATE CHANGED
PASSWORD/PIN	DATE CHANGED
📞	
NOTES	

VENDOR/WEBSITE	
USER NAME	
PASSWORD/PIN	DATE CHANGED
PASSWORD/PIN	DATE CHANGED
PASSWORD/PIN	DATE CHANGED
📞	
NOTES	

VENDOR/WEBSITE	
USER NAME	
PASSWORD/PIN	DATE CHANGED
PASSWORD/PIN	DATE CHANGED
PASSWORD/PIN	DATE CHANGED
📞	
NOTES	

VENDOR/WEBSITE	
USER NAME	
PASSWORD/PIN	DATE CHANGED
PASSWORD/PIN	DATE CHANGED
PASSWORD/PIN	DATE CHANGED
📞	
NOTES	

V

VENDOR/WEBSITE	
USER NAME	
PASSWORD/PIN	DATE CHANGED
PASSWORD/PIN	DATE CHANGED
PASSWORD/PIN	DATE CHANGED
📞	
NOTES	

VENDOR/WEBSITE	
USER NAME	
PASSWORD/PIN	DATE CHANGED
PASSWORD/PIN	DATE CHANGED
PASSWORD/PIN	DATE CHANGED
📞	
NOTES	

VENDOR/WEBSITE	
USER NAME	
PASSWORD/PIN	DATE CHANGED
PASSWORD/PIN	DATE CHANGED
PASSWORD/PIN	DATE CHANGED
📞	
NOTES	

VENDOR/WEBSITE	
USER NAME	
PASSWORD/PIN	DATE CHANGED
PASSWORD/PIN	DATE CHANGED
PASSWORD/PIN	DATE CHANGED
📞	
NOTES	

	V
VENDOR/WEBSITE	
USER NAME	
PASSWORD/PIN	DATE CHANGED
PASSWORD/PIN	DATE CHANGED
PASSWORD/PIN	DATE CHANGED
📞	
NOTES	
VENDOR/WEBSITE	
USER NAME	
PASSWORD/PIN	DATE CHANGED
PASSWORD/PIN	DATE CHANGED
PASSWORD/PIN	DATE CHANGED
📞	
NOTES	
VENDOR/WEBSITE	
USER NAME	
PASSWORD/PIN	DATE CHANGED
PASSWORD/PIN	DATE CHANGED
PASSWORD/PIN	DATE CHANGED
📞	
NOTES	
VENDOR/WEBSITE	
USER NAME	
PASSWORD/PIN	DATE CHANGED
PASSWORD/PIN	DATE CHANGED
PASSWORD/PIN	DATE CHANGED
📞	
NOTES	

V

VENDOR/WEBSITE	
USER NAME	
PASSWORD/PIN	DATE CHANGED
PASSWORD/PIN	DATE CHANGED
PASSWORD/PIN	DATE CHANGED
📞	
NOTES	

VENDOR/WEBSITE	
USER NAME	
PASSWORD/PIN	DATE CHANGED
PASSWORD/PIN	DATE CHANGED
PASSWORD/PIN	DATE CHANGED
📞	
NOTES	

VENDOR/WEBSITE	
USER NAME	
PASSWORD/PIN	DATE CHANGED
PASSWORD/PIN	DATE CHANGED
PASSWORD/PIN	DATE CHANGED
📞	
NOTES	

VENDOR/WEBSITE	
USER NAME	
PASSWORD/PIN	DATE CHANGED
PASSWORD/PIN	DATE CHANGED
PASSWORD/PIN	DATE CHANGED
📞	
NOTES	

	V
VENDOR/WEBSITE	
USER NAME	
PASSWORD/PIN	DATE CHANGED
PASSWORD/PIN	DATE CHANGED
PASSWORD/PIN	DATE CHANGED
NOTES	
VENDOR/WEBSITE	
USER NAME	
PASSWORD/PIN	DATE CHANGED
PASSWORD/PIN	DATE CHANGED
PASSWORD/PIN	DATE CHANGED
NOTES	
VENDOR/WEBSITE	
USER NAME	
PASSWORD/PIN	DATE CHANGED
PASSWORD/PIN	DATE CHANGED
PASSWORD/PIN	DATE CHANGED
NOTES	
VENDOR/WEBSITE	
USER NAME	
PASSWORD/PIN	DATE CHANGED
PASSWORD/PIN	DATE CHANGED
PASSWORD/PIN	DATE CHANGED
NOTES	

W

VENDOR/WEBSITE	
USER NAME	
PASSWORD/PIN	DATE CHANGED
PASSWORD/PIN	DATE CHANGED
PASSWORD/PIN	DATE CHANGED
📞	
NOTES	
VENDOR/WEBSITE	
USER NAME	
PASSWORD/PIN	DATE CHANGED
PASSWORD/PIN	DATE CHANGED
PASSWORD/PIN	DATE CHANGED
📞	
NOTES	
VENDOR/WEBSITE	
USER NAME	
PASSWORD/PIN	DATE CHANGED
PASSWORD/PIN	DATE CHANGED
PASSWORD/PIN	DATE CHANGED
📞	
NOTES	
VENDOR/WEBSITE	
USER NAME	
PASSWORD/PIN	DATE CHANGED
PASSWORD/PIN	DATE CHANGED
PASSWORD/PIN	DATE CHANGED
📞	
NOTES	

	W
VENDOR/WEBSITE	
USER NAME	
PASSWORD/PIN	DATE CHANGED
PASSWORD/PIN	DATE CHANGED
PASSWORD/PIN	DATE CHANGED
📞	
NOTES	
VENDOR/WEBSITE	
USER NAME	
PASSWORD/PIN	DATE CHANGED
PASSWORD/PIN	DATE CHANGED
PASSWORD/PIN	DATE CHANGED
📞	
NOTES	
VENDOR/WEBSITE	
USER NAME	
PASSWORD/PIN	DATE CHANGED
PASSWORD/PIN	DATE CHANGED
PASSWORD/PIN	DATE CHANGED
📞	
NOTES	
VENDOR/WEBSITE	
USER NAME	
PASSWORD/PIN	DATE CHANGED
PASSWORD/PIN	DATE CHANGED
PASSWORD/PIN	DATE CHANGED
📞	
NOTES	

W

VENDOR/WEBSITE	
USER NAME	
PASSWORD/PIN	DATE CHANGED
PASSWORD/PIN	DATE CHANGED
PASSWORD/PIN	DATE CHANGED
📞	
NOTES	

VENDOR/WEBSITE	
USER NAME	
PASSWORD/PIN	DATE CHANGED
PASSWORD/PIN	DATE CHANGED
PASSWORD/PIN	DATE CHANGED
📞	
NOTES	

VENDOR/WEBSITE	
USER NAME	
PASSWORD/PIN	DATE CHANGED
PASSWORD/PIN	DATE CHANGED
PASSWORD/PIN	DATE CHANGED
📞	
NOTES	

VENDOR/WEBSITE	
USER NAME	
PASSWORD/PIN	DATE CHANGED
PASSWORD/PIN	DATE CHANGED
PASSWORD/PIN	DATE CHANGED
📞	
NOTES	

	W
VENDOR/WEBSITE	
USER NAME	
PASSWORD/PIN	DATE CHANGED
PASSWORD/PIN	DATE CHANGED
PASSWORD/PIN	DATE CHANGED
NOTES	
VENDOR/WEBSITE	
USER NAME	
PASSWORD/PIN	DATE CHANGED
PASSWORD/PIN	DATE CHANGED
PASSWORD/PIN	DATE CHANGED
NOTES	
VENDOR/WEBSITE	
USER NAME	
PASSWORD/PIN	DATE CHANGED
PASSWORD/PIN	DATE CHANGED
PASSWORD/PIN	DATE CHANGED
NOTES	
VENDOR/WEBSITE	
USER NAME	
PASSWORD/PIN	DATE CHANGED
PASSWORD/PIN	DATE CHANGED
PASSWORD/PIN	DATE CHANGED
NOTES	

X

VENDOR/WEBSITE	
USER NAME	
PASSWORD/PIN	DATE CHANGED
PASSWORD/PIN	DATE CHANGED
PASSWORD/PIN	DATE CHANGED
☎	
NOTES	

VENDOR/WEBSITE	
USER NAME	
PASSWORD/PIN	DATE CHANGED
PASSWORD/PIN	DATE CHANGED
PASSWORD/PIN	DATE CHANGED
☎	
NOTES	

VENDOR/WEBSITE	
USER NAME	
PASSWORD/PIN	DATE CHANGED
PASSWORD/PIN	DATE CHANGED
PASSWORD/PIN	DATE CHANGED
☎	
NOTES	

VENDOR/WEBSITE	
USER NAME	
PASSWORD/PIN	DATE CHANGED
PASSWORD/PIN	DATE CHANGED
PASSWORD/PIN	DATE CHANGED
☎	
NOTES	

VENDOR/WEBSITE	
USER NAME	
PASSWORD/PIN	DATE CHANGED
PASSWORD/PIN	DATE CHANGED
PASSWORD/PIN	DATE CHANGED
📞	
NOTES	

VENDOR/WEBSITE	
USER NAME	
PASSWORD/PIN	DATE CHANGED
PASSWORD/PIN	DATE CHANGED
PASSWORD/PIN	DATE CHANGED
📞	
NOTES	

VENDOR/WEBSITE	
USER NAME	
PASSWORD/PIN	DATE CHANGED
PASSWORD/PIN	DATE CHANGED
PASSWORD/PIN	DATE CHANGED
📞	
NOTES	

VENDOR/WEBSITE	
USER NAME	
PASSWORD/PIN	DATE CHANGED
PASSWORD/PIN	DATE CHANGED
PASSWORD/PIN	DATE CHANGED
📞	
NOTES	

X

VENDOR/WEBSITE	
USER NAME	
PASSWORD/PIN	DATE CHANGED
PASSWORD/PIN	DATE CHANGED
PASSWORD/PIN	DATE CHANGED
📞	
NOTES	

VENDOR/WEBSITE	
USER NAME	
PASSWORD/PIN	DATE CHANGED
PASSWORD/PIN	DATE CHANGED
PASSWORD/PIN	DATE CHANGED
📞	
NOTES	

VENDOR/WEBSITE	
USER NAME	
PASSWORD/PIN	DATE CHANGED
PASSWORD/PIN	DATE CHANGED
PASSWORD/PIN	DATE CHANGED
📞	
NOTES	

VENDOR/WEBSITE	
USER NAME	
PASSWORD/PIN	DATE CHANGED
PASSWORD/PIN	DATE CHANGED
PASSWORD/PIN	DATE CHANGED
📞	
NOTES	

	X
VENDOR/WEBSITE	
USER NAME	
PASSWORD/PIN	DATE CHANGED
PASSWORD/PIN	DATE CHANGED
PASSWORD/PIN	DATE CHANGED
☎	
NOTES	
VENDOR/WEBSITE	
USER NAME	
PASSWORD/PIN	DATE CHANGED
PASSWORD/PIN	DATE CHANGED
PASSWORD/PIN	DATE CHANGED
☎	
NOTES	
VENDOR/WEBSITE	
USER NAME	
PASSWORD/PIN	DATE CHANGED
PASSWORD/PIN	DATE CHANGED
PASSWORD/PIN	DATE CHANGED
☎	
NOTES	
VENDOR/WEBSITE	
USER NAME	
PASSWORD/PIN	DATE CHANGED
PASSWORD/PIN	DATE CHANGED
PASSWORD/PIN	DATE CHANGED
☎	
NOTES	

X

VENDOR/WEBSITE	
USER NAME	
PASSWORD/PIN	DATE CHANGED
PASSWORD/PIN	DATE CHANGED
PASSWORD/PIN	DATE CHANGED
📞	
NOTES	

VENDOR/WEBSITE	
USER NAME	
PASSWORD/PIN	DATE CHANGED
PASSWORD/PIN	DATE CHANGED
PASSWORD/PIN	DATE CHANGED
📞	
NOTES	

VENDOR/WEBSITE	
USER NAME	
PASSWORD/PIN	DATE CHANGED
PASSWORD/PIN	DATE CHANGED
PASSWORD/PIN	DATE CHANGED
📞	
NOTES	

VENDOR/WEBSITE	
USER NAME	
PASSWORD/PIN	DATE CHANGED
PASSWORD/PIN	DATE CHANGED
PASSWORD/PIN	DATE CHANGED
📞	
NOTES	

	X
VENDOR/WEBSITE	
USER NAME	
PASSWORD/PIN	DATE CHANGED
PASSWORD/PIN	DATE CHANGED
PASSWORD/PIN	DATE CHANGED
📞	
NOTES	
VENDOR/WEBSITE	
USER NAME	
PASSWORD/PIN	DATE CHANGED
PASSWORD/PIN	DATE CHANGED
PASSWORD/PIN	DATE CHANGED
📞	
NOTES	
VENDOR/WEBSITE	
USER NAME	
PASSWORD/PIN	DATE CHANGED
PASSWORD/PIN	DATE CHANGED
PASSWORD/PIN	DATE CHANGED
📞	
NOTES	
VENDOR/WEBSITE	
USER NAME	
PASSWORD/PIN	DATE CHANGED
PASSWORD/PIN	DATE CHANGED
PASSWORD/PIN	DATE CHANGED
📞	
NOTES	

Y

VENDOR/WEBSITE	
USER NAME	
PASSWORD/PIN	DATE CHANGED
PASSWORD/PIN	DATE CHANGED
PASSWORD/PIN	DATE CHANGED
📞	
NOTES	

VENDOR/WEBSITE	
USER NAME	
PASSWORD/PIN	DATE CHANGED
PASSWORD/PIN	DATE CHANGED
PASSWORD/PIN	DATE CHANGED
📞	
NOTES	

VENDOR/WEBSITE	
USER NAME	
PASSWORD/PIN	DATE CHANGED
PASSWORD/PIN	DATE CHANGED
PASSWORD/PIN	DATE CHANGED
📞	
NOTES	

VENDOR/WEBSITE	
USER NAME	
PASSWORD/PIN	DATE CHANGED
PASSWORD/PIN	DATE CHANGED
PASSWORD/PIN	DATE CHANGED
📞	
NOTES	

	Y
VENDOR/WEBSITE	
USER NAME	
PASSWORD/PIN	DATE CHANGED
PASSWORD/PIN	DATE CHANGED
PASSWORD/PIN	DATE CHANGED
📞	
NOTES	
VENDOR/WEBSITE	
USER NAME	
PASSWORD/PIN	DATE CHANGED
PASSWORD/PIN	DATE CHANGED
PASSWORD/PIN	DATE CHANGED
📞	
NOTES	
VENDOR/WEBSITE	
USER NAME	
PASSWORD/PIN	DATE CHANGED
PASSWORD/PIN	DATE CHANGED
PASSWORD/PIN	DATE CHANGED
📞	
NOTES	
VENDOR/WEBSITE	
USER NAME	
PASSWORD/PIN	DATE CHANGED
PASSWORD/PIN	DATE CHANGED
PASSWORD/PIN	DATE CHANGED
📞	
NOTES	

Y

VENDOR/WEBSITE	
USER NAME	
PASSWORD/PIN	DATE CHANGED
PASSWORD/PIN	DATE CHANGED
PASSWORD/PIN	DATE CHANGED
☎	
NOTES	

VENDOR/WEBSITE	
USER NAME	
PASSWORD/PIN	DATE CHANGED
PASSWORD/PIN	DATE CHANGED
PASSWORD/PIN	DATE CHANGED
☎	
NOTES	

VENDOR/WEBSITE	
USER NAME	
PASSWORD/PIN	DATE CHANGED
PASSWORD/PIN	DATE CHANGED
PASSWORD/PIN	DATE CHANGED
☎	
NOTES	

VENDOR/WEBSITE	
USER NAME	
PASSWORD/PIN	DATE CHANGED
PASSWORD/PIN	DATE CHANGED
PASSWORD/PIN	DATE CHANGED
☎	
NOTES	

	Y
VENDOR/WEBSITE	
USER NAME	
PASSWORD/PIN	DATE CHANGED
PASSWORD/PIN	DATE CHANGED
PASSWORD/PIN	DATE CHANGED
📞	
NOTES	
VENDOR/WEBSITE	
USER NAME	
PASSWORD/PIN	DATE CHANGED
PASSWORD/PIN	DATE CHANGED
PASSWORD/PIN	DATE CHANGED
📞	
NOTES	
VENDOR/WEBSITE	
USER NAME	
PASSWORD/PIN	DATE CHANGED
PASSWORD/PIN	DATE CHANGED
PASSWORD/PIN	DATE CHANGED
📞	
NOTES	
VENDOR/WEBSITE	
USER NAME	
PASSWORD/PIN	DATE CHANGED
PASSWORD/PIN	DATE CHANGED
PASSWORD/PIN	DATE CHANGED
📞	
NOTES	

Z

VENDOR/WEBSITE	
USER NAME	
PASSWORD/PIN	DATE CHANGED
PASSWORD/PIN	DATE CHANGED
PASSWORD/PIN	DATE CHANGED
📞	
NOTES	

VENDOR/WEBSITE	
USER NAME	
PASSWORD/PIN	DATE CHANGED
PASSWORD/PIN	DATE CHANGED
PASSWORD/PIN	DATE CHANGED
📞	
NOTES	

VENDOR/WEBSITE	
USER NAME	
PASSWORD/PIN	DATE CHANGED
PASSWORD/PIN	DATE CHANGED
PASSWORD/PIN	DATE CHANGED
📞	
NOTES	

VENDOR/WEBSITE	
USER NAME	
PASSWORD/PIN	DATE CHANGED
PASSWORD/PIN	DATE CHANGED
PASSWORD/PIN	DATE CHANGED
📞	
NOTES	

VENDOR/WEBSITE	
USER NAME	
PASSWORD/PIN	DATE CHANGED
PASSWORD/PIN	DATE CHANGED
PASSWORD/PIN	DATE CHANGED
📞	
NOTES	
VENDOR/WEBSITE	
USER NAME	
PASSWORD/PIN	DATE CHANGED
PASSWORD/PIN	DATE CHANGED
PASSWORD/PIN	DATE CHANGED
📞	
NOTES	
VENDOR/WEBSITE	
USER NAME	
PASSWORD/PIN	DATE CHANGED
PASSWORD/PIN	DATE CHANGED
PASSWORD/PIN	DATE CHANGED
📞	
NOTES	
VENDOR/WEBSITE	
USER NAME	
PASSWORD/PIN	DATE CHANGED
PASSWORD/PIN	DATE CHANGED
PASSWORD/PIN	DATE CHANGED
📞	
NOTES	

Z

VENDOR/WEBSITE	
USER NAME	
PASSWORD/PIN	DATE CHANGED
PASSWORD/PIN	DATE CHANGED
PASSWORD/PIN	DATE CHANGED
📞	
NOTES	
VENDOR/WEBSITE	
USER NAME	
PASSWORD/PIN	DATE CHANGED
PASSWORD/PIN	DATE CHANGED
PASSWORD/PIN	DATE CHANGED
📞	
NOTES	
VENDOR/WEBSITE	
USER NAME	
PASSWORD/PIN	DATE CHANGED
PASSWORD/PIN	DATE CHANGED
PASSWORD/PIN	DATE CHANGED
📞	
NOTES	
VENDOR/WEBSITE	
USER NAME	
PASSWORD/PIN	DATE CHANGED
PASSWORD/PIN	DATE CHANGED
PASSWORD/PIN	DATE CHANGED
📞	
NOTES	

	Z
VENDOR/WEBSITE	
USER NAME	
PASSWORD/PIN	DATE CHANGED
PASSWORD/PIN	DATE CHANGED
PASSWORD/PIN	DATE CHANGED
📞	
NOTES	
VENDOR/WEBSITE	
USER NAME	
PASSWORD/PIN	DATE CHANGED
PASSWORD/PIN	DATE CHANGED
PASSWORD/PIN	DATE CHANGED
📞	
NOTES	
VENDOR/WEBSITE	
USER NAME	
PASSWORD/PIN	DATE CHANGED
PASSWORD/PIN	DATE CHANGED
PASSWORD/PIN	DATE CHANGED
📞	
NOTES	
VENDOR/WEBSITE	
USER NAME	
PASSWORD/PIN	DATE CHANGED
PASSWORD/PIN	DATE CHANGED
PASSWORD/PIN	DATE CHANGED
📞	
NOTES	

VERY IMPORTANT PAGES

USEFUL INTERNET & COMPUTER INFORMATION

INTERNET SERVICE PROVIDER (ISP)

NAME:

WEBSITE LOGIN:

WEBSITE PASSWORD:

TECH SUPPORT TEL:

TECH SUPPORT EMAIL:

CUSTOMER SERVICE TEL:

CUSTOMER SERVICE EMAIL:

WEB HOST

NAME:

WEBSITE LOGIN:

WEBSITE PASSWORD:

TECH SUPPORT TEL:

TECH SUPPORT EMAIL:

CUSTOMER SERVICE TEL:

CUSTOMER SERVICE EMAIL:

EMAIL (WORK)

MAIL SERVER TYPE:

INCOMING SERVER:

OUTGOING SERVER:

USERNAME:

PASSWORD:

EMAIL (PERSONAL)

MAIL SERVER TYPE:

INCOMING SERVER:

OUTGOING SERVER:

USERNAME:

PASSWORD:

OTHER

HOME NETWORK SETTINGS

BROADBAND MODEM

MODEL:

SERIAL NUMBER:

MAC ADDRESS:

ADMINISTRATION URL/IP ADDRESS:

WAN IP ADDRESS:

USERNAME:

PASSWORD:

ROUTER WIRELESS ACCESS POINT

MODEL:

SERIAL NUMBER:

FACTORY DEFAULT ADMIN IP ADDRESS:

FACTORY DEFAULT USER NAME:

FACTORY DEFAULT PASSWORD:

NEW ADMIN IP ADDRESS:

NEW USERNAME:

NEW PASSWORD:

WAN SETTINGS

MAC ADDRESS: (SEE BROADBAND MODEM)

IP ADDRESS: (SEE BROADBAND MODEM)

HOST NAME: (IF REQUIRED BY ISP)

DOMAIN NAME: (IF REQUIRED BY ISP

SUBNET MASK:

DEFAULT GATEWAY:

DNS – PRIMARY:

DNS – SECONDARY:

LAN (NETWORK SETTINGS)

IP ADDRESS:

SUBNET MASK:

DHCP RANGE: (IF DHCP ENABLED)

WIRELESS SETTINGS (WIFI, WLAN)

SSID: (WIRELESS NETWORK NAME)

CHANNEL:

SECURITY MODE:

SHARED KEY: (FOR WPA)

PASSPHRASE: (FOR WEP)

ADDITIONAL NOTES